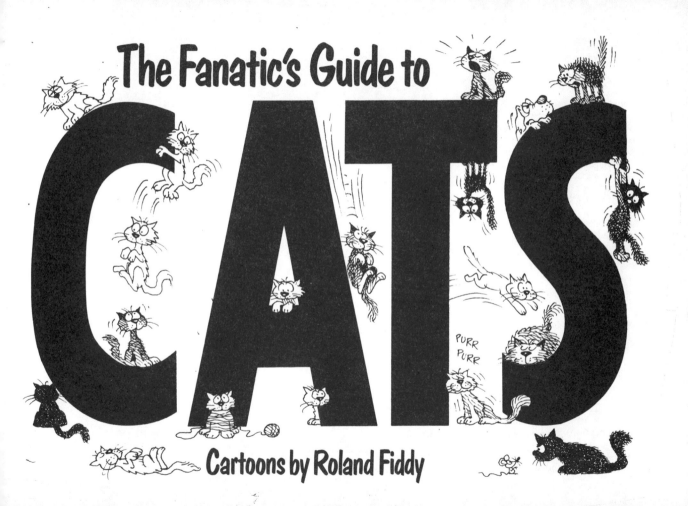

The Fanatic's Guide to CATS

Cartoons by Roland Fiddy

In the same series:
The Fanatic's Guide to Computers
The Fanatic's Guide to Dads
The Fanatic's Guide to Diets
The Fanatic's Guide to Dogs
The Fanatic's Guide to Golf
The Fanatic's Guide to Men
The Fanatic's Guide to Money
The Fanatic's Guide to Sex

First published in Great Britain in 1990 by
**Exley Publications Ltd, 16 Chalk Hill,
Watford, Herts WD1 4BN, United Kingdom.**

Second and third printings 1991
Fourth printing 1992

ISBN 1-85015-237-3

A copy of the CIP data is available from the
British Library on request.

Typeset by Brush Off Studios, St Albans, Herts AL3 4PH.
Printed and bound in Hungary.

Roland Fiddy

Roland Fiddy, Cartoonist.

Born in Plymouth, Devon. Studied art at Plymouth and Bristol Colleges of Art. Works as a freelance cartoonist and illustrator. His cartoons have been published in Britain, the United States, and many other countries. Has taken part in International Cartoon Festivals since 1984, and has won the following awards.

1984 Special Prize, Yomiuri Shimbun, Tokyo.

1984 First Prize, Beringen International Cartoon Exhibition, Belgium

1984 Prize of the Public, Netherlands Cartoon Festival.

1985 First Prize, Netherlands Cartoon Festival

1985 "Silver Hat" (Second Prize) Knokke-Heist International Cartoon Festival, Belgium.

1986 First Prize, Beringen International Cartoon Exhibition, Belgium

1986 First Prize, Netherlands Cartoon Festival

1986 First Prize, Sofia Cartoon Exhibition, Bulgaria.

1987 Second Prize, World Cartoon Gallery, Skopje, Yugoslavia.

1987 "Casino Prize" Knokke-Heist International Cartoon Festival, Belgium

1987 UNESCO Prize, Gabrovo International Cartoon Biennial, Bulgaria.

1987 First Prize, Piracicaba International Humour Exhibition, Brazil.

1988 "Golden Date" award, International Salon of Humour, Bordighera, Italy.

1988 Second Prize, Berol Cartoon Awards, London, England.

1989 E.E.C. Prize, European Cartoon Exhibition, Kruishoutem, Belgium.

1989 Press Prize, Gabrovo International Cartoon Biennial, Bulgaria.

1990 First Prize, Knokke-Heist International Cartoon Festival, Belgium.

1991 Prize for Excellence, Yomiuri Shimbun, Tokyo.

Cats are Cacophonous

①

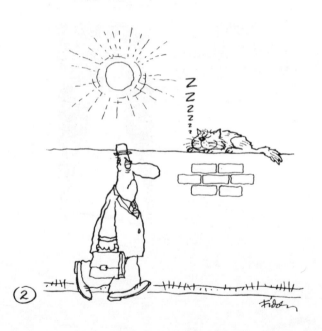

②

Some cats are corpulent

Cats are Cheerful

①

②

R-R-RING!
R-R-RING!

①

②

⑤

④

HISSSSS!! GRRRRR!!

③

Cats are Carnivorous

Cats are Cumulative

Cats are Cuddly

④

PURRR
PURRR
PURRR
PURRR

③

Cats are Clever

Cats are Cosseted

Cats are Choosy

Cats can be Compassionate

Cats are Curious

Cats are Claustrophobic

Cats are Clairvoyant

Cats are Companionable

②

Most cats are Caudate*

* having a tail

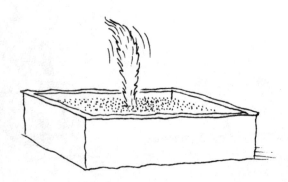

Fiddy

②

①

②

Cats can be Confusing

Cats can appear contemptuous

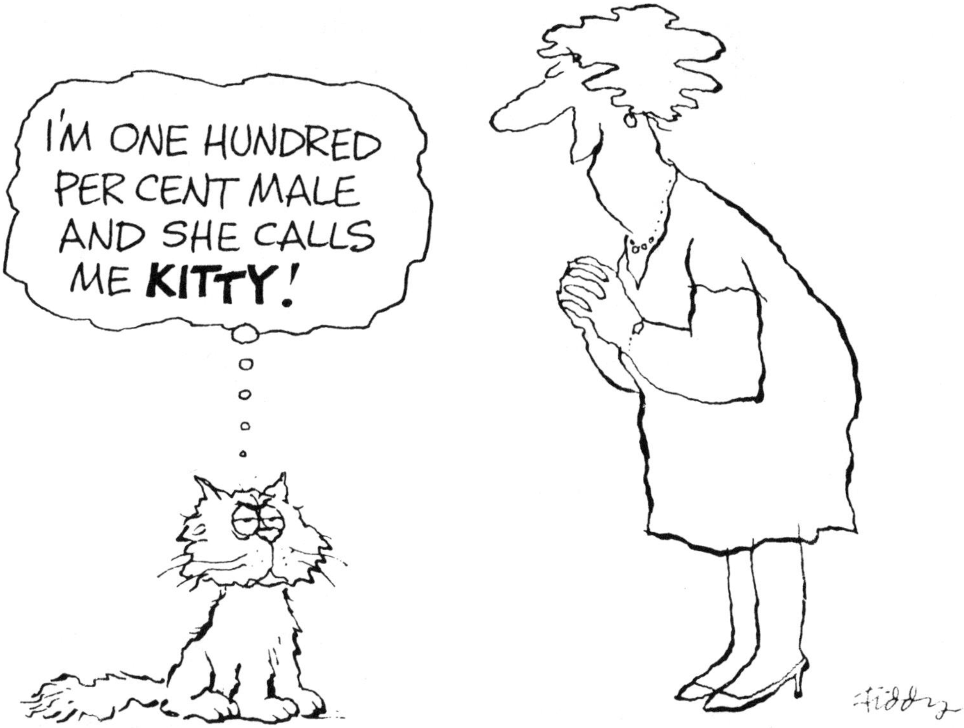
I'M ONE HUNDRED PER CENT MALE AND SHE CALLS ME **KITTY**!